AN EXPLOSION OF TASTE. **OLÉ Olives!**

www.oliveit.eu

SIMON &
SCHUSTER
ILLUSTRATED

London · New York · Sydney · Toronto · New Delhi

A CBS COMPANY

First published in Great Britain by
Simon & Schuster UK Ltd, 2014
A CBS Company

Text and photographs copyright
© Olive it! UK, 2014
Design copyright
© Simon & Schuster UK Ltd, 2014

SIMON & SCHUSTER
ILLUSTRATED BOOKS
Simon & Schuster UK Ltd
222 Gray's Inn Road
London WC1X 8HB
www.simonandschuster.co.uk

Simon & Schuster Australia, Sydney
Simon & Schuster India, New Delhi

10 9 8 7 6 5 4 3 2 1

A CIP catalogue record for this book is available from the British Library
ISBN 978-1-47113-451-7

Design and art direction: Corinna Farrow and Sally Bond
Food photography: William Shaw
Photograph of Omar Allibhoy: Tony Briggs
Photograph of José Pizarro and his parents:
From *Seasonal Spanish Food* by José Pizarro, published by Kyle Books, priced £15.99. Photography: Emma Lee
Photograph of Sue Ashworth: William Shaw
Recipe development: Sue Ashworth
Home economy: Mitzie Wilson
Project managers: Anna Robinson and Lorraine Jerram
Director of Illustrated Publishing: Ami Stewart
For Storm Communications: Susan Maskell and Catherine Mallaband

Additional images © Stockdisc™ (www.stockdisc.com)

Colour reproduction by Dot Gradations Ltd, UK
Printed and bound in Germany

AN EXPLOSION OF TASTE. OLÉ Olives!
www.oliveit.eu

contents

the OLIVE it! campaign

The Olive it! campaign is a celebration of table olives and is designed to inspire you and take you on a journey of discovery. The European campaign is being run in the UK, as well as in Spain and France, to appeal to olive lovers far and wide.

Olive it! is an innovative culinary concept that demonstrates how a simple olive can spark your imagination and awaken new taste sensations. By seasoning olives in a number of different ways we will uncover new aromas and flavours, inspired by the Mediterranean, and show you how easy it is to create a delicious dish within minutes.

Whether green, black or mixed, table olives are flavoursome and unique, containing as they do four basic flavours: bitter, sweet, salt and sour. On their own they are great as a delicious snack but when seasoned with new and inventive combinations of ingredients they can produce a true explosion of taste. From seasoning with classic ingredients such as capers, cheese or peppers, to more daring ingredients including ginger, soy sauce and wasabi, the possibilities to experiment and enjoy olives are endless.

This campaign will show you some of these unique combinations from recognised chefs and culinary experts and encourage you to have a go yourself and be creative in the kitchen. All the recipes contained in this book are easy to follow and can be made within minutes by everyone – irrespective of age or cooking experience.

As well as demonstrating the versatility of the humble olive, the Olive it! campaign will also be highlighting the nutritional value of olives and their role within the Mediterranean way of life. Olives are central to the Mediterranean diet and social gatherings, and we will be exploring why millions of people around the world are fans of table olives and what makes them so special. Whether you are hosting a formal event or work gathering, having a romantic dinner for two or holding a party for friends and family, olives can be enjoyed on all occasions.

Keep in touch with our campaign by visiting our website at **www.oliveit.eu**, following us at **@Oliveit_UK** and liking our facebook page, **www.facebook.com/oliveit_uk**

...there are hundreds of ways to enjoy olives

Enjoying good-quality food with friends and family is so important. Whether it's an impromptu get-together or to mark a special occasion, sharing good times with loved ones over tasty food and drink can bring much love, laughter and happiness.

Socialising over food is central to the Mediterranean way of life and was a big part of my family culture when I was growing up in Madrid. A love of cooking runs in my family. My mum was a fabulous baker. She was a great inspiration to me as she entertained and cooked for large numbers. The delicious aromas from the kitchen made it seem cool, and at five years old I was whisking eggs and producing my first recipe – a flan.

By eight I was selling puddings to neighbours during the summer holidays and I haven't looked back since. Inspiring people to try new flavours and combine simple but delicious ingredients to create fantastic meals is something I love doing, which is why I'm delighted to be involved in the Olive it! campaign.

Olives play an integral role in Mediterranean cuisine – indeed, where would it be without them! Loved by all generations, olives are part of our culture and history, and are one of my favourite foods. And they don't just taste great on their own; there are hundreds of ways to enjoy olives. Whether they are whole or pitted or combined with other great-tasting ingredients, they can create a simple yet mouth-watering dish that everyone will enjoy.

Cooking with olives can be fun and exciting, and we hope this book will inspire you in the kitchen and encourage you to create these quick, easy and delicious recipes at home for your loved ones. Enjoy preparing simple marinades, tapas and tapenades and along the way learn about the history of olives, their role and influence in today's Mediterranean culture, their nutritional value and what makes them so great.

We've also included some special recipes from me and my friends, José Pizarro and Sue Ashworth.

I hope you enjoy the book, and my recipe overleaf, and have fun discovering the versatility and joy of olives!

Omar Allibhoy

Omar Allibhoy

1 jar of queen olives

6 garlic cloves

1 fresh red chilli

1 teaspoon cumin seeds

1 tablespoon sweet pimentón

100 ml mild olive oil

Drain the olives from the brine and place them in a glass jar.

Crush the garlic cloves with the skin, slice the chilli in half lengthways and crush the cumin seeds with the side of a knife. Add to the jar with the pimentón and olive oil.

Stir everything together well (or put on the lid and shake the jar, if you prefer) and nibble straight away.

The olives can be kept in the fridge in an airtight container for up to 2 weeks.

Serves 4

green olives with sweet pimentón, cumin, red chilli and garlic

...olives have always played an important role in my life

Cooking with simple and uncomplicated ingredients is key to my philosophy. Nothing is better than bringing together a few ingredients to create bright, vibrant flavours that everyone will love. I am delighted, therefore, to be involved in the Olive it! campaign, which celebrates one of my favourite foods and explores different ways of enjoying and cooking with olives.

Olives are one of those special ingredients that I love. Delicious on their own, they are also highly versatile and nutritious, and can take dishes to new heights. Simple and classic, they can turn a standard dish into something sophisticated and full of flavour.

I grew up in Extremadura and olives have always played an important role in my life. We lived on a farm and I used to help my dad pick olives first thing in the morning. I would then help my mum to marinate and cook with olives – I can still smell the wonderful aromas that came from the kitchen and taste the mouth-watering flavours that started my love affair with olives.

After living and working in the UK for 14 years, I have continued on my food journey and love sharing with others my passion for great-tasting food. My cooking is inspired by my homeland and based on traditional recipes but with a modern twist.

Here in the UK we have an appetite for fabulous food but often overlook olives, or we see them just as a healthy snack, when in fact they can be so much more. I hope this campaign inspires people to experiment with olives and try new serving suggestions.

The recipe I would like to share with you here is called Olives Isabel – a beautiful dish of Manzanilla olives marinated my mum's way. This dish reminds me of home and is very special to me. Bursting with flavour, it is simple and easy to recreate at home. Try it with a glass of dry sherry before lunch or dinner as a delicious treat.

I hope this recipe and the others in this wonderful cookbook bring you much enjoyment as you discover new ways of cooking and preparing olives. Don't forget to follow the campaign on **www.oliveit.eu** for more recipe ideas from the team and myself.

José Pizarro

José Pizarro

75 g black olives

75 g 'turning colour' olives

75 g Manzanilla olives

2 whole garlic cloves, skins removed

grated zest of 1 orange

2 tablespoons extra virgin olive oil

1 bay leaf

¼ teaspoon chilli flakes

¼ teaspoon black peppercorns, roughly crushed

Mix all the ingredients in a large bowl and leave to marinate for 3–4 hours (or overnight) in the fridge.

Allow to come to room temperature before serving.

Serves 4

olives isabel
(olives marinated my mum's way)

a brief history of olives

THEIR ORIGINS

Olives have a rich history. The olive tree has been in existence for millennia, with ancient texts documenting its role as an invaluable natural resource and underlining the historical significance of olives as a food source.

Widely cultivated across the Mediterranean, Africa and Asia Minor, olives were historically considered as a symbol of peace, wisdom and progress.

The Mediterranean has a long tradition when it comes to growing olive trees and harvesting their fruit, which is why olives are one of the most traditional and important foods in the Mediterranean diet and play a central role in the region's gastronomic heritage. The fruit is also of major agricultural importance in the region as the source of olive oil.

THE STORY SO FAR

According to the data of the International Olive Council, Spain is the main olive-producing country in the world, considerably ahead of other countries in the Mediterranean. The country was also the first to export olives internationally, with Spanish colonisers transporting olives to the New World in the 16th century.

Today there are around 850 million olive trees on earth, covering more than 10 million hectares of land. Andalucía and Extremadura are the main growing regions but there are lots of smaller areas where olives are grown.

In recent years our love of olives has grown massively, with the average world production up to 2,371 tons during the last five harvest seasons, out of which 25% were produced in Spain, representing 39% of the global trade in 2012.

According to the data of the Spanish Directorate of Customs, table olives exported by Spain in 2012, including to European Union countries, reached 323.691 tons (net weight), with a value of approximately 630.6 million euros. The main destinations in volume terms are the USA, Italy, Russia, France, Germany, Portugal, Saudi Arabia, Brazil, Canada and the UK.

This history, combined with the warm Mediterranean climate and modern processing methods, makes olives from the region some of the most delicious in the world.

TYPES Olives are loved around the world for their delicious taste, versatility and nutritional benefits.

Out of the many types of olive trees that can be found, the majority are used to obtain oil. Only a few are suitable for the production of table olives, which will depend on factors such as the quantity of fat contained in the fruit, the size of the olive pit relative to the pulp and how easy it is to detach it, and the characteristics of the olive peel.

The perfect table olive will have a medium fat content, a small, smooth pit that can be easily detached, a delicately flavoured firm pulp and thin peel. The olive varieties that most match these characteristics are Manzanilla and Gordal, together with Hojiblanca and Cacerena (which are also used to produce oil). There are other local varieties such as Alorena, Carrasquena, Morona and Verdial.

COLOUR Olives can also be classified according to their colour. Rather than signifying type, the different colour tones represent the level of ripeness when plucked from the olive tree.

Very green olives are obtained from the fruits harvested at the optimal ripening stage. The colouring of the fruit may vary slightly from green to fair yellow.
Mixed olives are pink or maroon in colour and are harvested before being fully ripened. These 'turning colour' olives are midway through their life cycle and offer yet another exciting variation in terms of taste and texture.
Natural black olives are obtained from the fruits harvested when they reach their full

olives today

ripening stage, or just before. They can be a black or reddish colour, a violet black, deep violet or greenish black depending on the production area and time of harvesting. **Black olives** are obtained from the fruits when ripening is accelerated. They lose their bitterness as a result of the treatment process.

HARVESTING

Olives are picked in the months of September and October, when the fruit reaches the right size and just before it starts to change colour. Most table olives are picked in the traditional way, one by one, in order to avoid damaging the fruit. Then the olives are transported, handled and prepared using modern facilities and state-of-the-art technology.

Table olives have great economic and social importance. The care and attention bestowed on trees that are used to produce table olives, and the hand-picking that takes place once the olives reach full ripeness, give an idea of how labour-intensive the process is. And this is equally true once the olives go into commercial production, where similar manpower needs prevail in the areas of seasoning, selection, classification, pitting, stuffing and packaging.

FILLINGS

Some of the most popular stuffing ingredients include:

Garlic • Anchovies • Pimento or red pepper • Almonds • Cheese

However, you can find more than 80 stuffings, including salmon, tuna, lemon, orange, ham, seaweed and chorizo.

olives – the healthy facts

DR SIMON POOLE,
GP AND AUTHOR

For thousands of years the peoples of the Mediterranean have shaped the landscape with the cultivation of the olive tree, renowned for the unique nutritional qualities of its fruit.

The many benefits of the Mediterranean diet have been demonstrated through numerous studies, and it has recently been declared an 'Intangible Cultural Heritage of Humanity'. In countries where the diet is consumed, heart disease rates are significantly lower, due in no small part to the greater consumption of products that are rich in monounsaturated fatty acids.

Table olives are an integral part of Mediterranean cuisine, particularly valued for adding flavour, texture and goodness to recipes, snacks and appetisers. Embedded in the culture of the region, they are the origin of olive oil and are virtually cholesterol free, with an energy level of around 150 calories per 100 g (or approximately 37 calories for seven olives).

Olives contain monounsaturated fats. Up to 77% of the fat content of olives is oleic acid – a monounsaturated fat. Studies show that replacing saturated fats with unsaturated fats can help maintain normal blood cholesterol levels, and olives are an excellent source of these healthy fats.

Table olives are also a good natural source of vitamin E, which helps protect cells from free radicals, and black olives in particular are a good source of iron too, providing some 45.5% of the recommended daily allowance.

Check out the table on the left for the full nutritional benefits of green and black olives.

HAPPY EATING!

Nutritional composition of green olives and black olives

(100 g edible portion)	Green olive	Black olive
Energy (kcal)	154	143
Proteins (g)	1.1	0.6
Carbohydrates (g)	0	0.075
Total Fat (g)	16.3	15.4
Saturated Fat (g)	3.23	2.7
Monounsaturated Fat (g)	11	11
Polyunsaturated Fat (g)	1.4	0.85
Cholesterol (mg)	0.2	0.25
Fibre (g)	2.6	2.6
Sodium (g)	1.5	0.77
Vitamin A (Retinol)	6 (% RDA)	4 (% RDA)
Vitamin E (Tocopherol)	33 (% RDA)	31.75 (% RDA)
Vitamin C (Ascorbic Acid)	0.7 (% RDA)	0 (% RDA)
Calcium	6 (% RDA)	6.5 (% RDA)
Phosphorus	1 (% RDA)	1 (% RDA)
Iron	4 (% RDA)	45.5 (% RDA)
Magnesium	4.3 (% RDA)	2.5 (% RDA)
Zinc	1.6 (% RDA)	2 (% RDA)

Source: Fats Institute of Seville. Spanish National Research Council. Reference values for nutritional labelling, 2006.

> ...I adore olives,
> with their wonderful
> hues and flavours

I love olives. Yet I have to be really honest – I didn't always. As a child I would try the lonely black olive in the middle of a pizza. I was determined that I would (and should) like it, though I'd wrinkle my nose and wonder why it was there – other than as a cursory garnish.

But now it's completely different: I adore olives, with their wonderful hues and flavours. I use them in a multitude of different dishes, from simple starters and tapas to salads, fish dishes and mouth-watering meat meals. One of my Sunday dinner favourites is slow-braised Mediterranean-style brisket of beef, cooked for hours in full-bodied red wine with sultanas, celery, onions, garlic and stock with black olives and thyme. It's divine. And for a quick meal, I love a warm Niçoise salad with seared fresh tuna steak, with both green and black olives. Heaven!

The legendary Keith Floyd was a great influence on me. I was recipe writer for his book *Floyd on Spain* a few years ago, and it threw me into testing and creating new ideas for how to use olives in all kinds of ways. That experience led me to working with Weight Watchers, so how could I resist one of my best-loved tips for keeping an eye on your waistline? Just enjoy a small bowl of olives before your meal to curb your appetite – then you won't overeat (and you'll enjoy the olives, too!).

I hope you'll experiment with the great flavour combinations within these pages, so that you'll discover the versatility of olives and see them in a bright new light. Even better – every time you have a lovely bowl of perfect olives (maybe with a little tipple?) you can imagine you're chilling out with sundown cocktails at a beachfront café, or having fun at a tapas bar in Barcelona. No wonder we love olives!

Sue Ashworth

marinades, tapenades and tapas

Drain the olives from the brine and place them in a bowl.

Put the vinegar into a saucepan. Pare three or four strips of zest from the orange, using a sharp knife or potato peeler. Slice these into fine shreds and add them to the vinegar with the bay leaves. Squeeze the juice from the orange and add to the saucepan. Heat and simmer over a very low heat until the liquid has reduced by about half.

Stir the olive oil and honey into the vinegar and orange mixture, then pour over the olives. Add the figs and stir together gently, then leave to marinate for 20–30 minutes before serving. Alternatively, cover and refrigerate for up to 3 hours, though serve at room temperature for the best flavour.

1 jar or tin of green olives

100 ml white wine vinegar

1 orange

2 fresh bay leaves, torn in half

50 ml olive oil

2 tablespoons lavender honey or clear honey

3 ripe figs, sliced

Serves 4

green olives marinated with figs, orange and bay

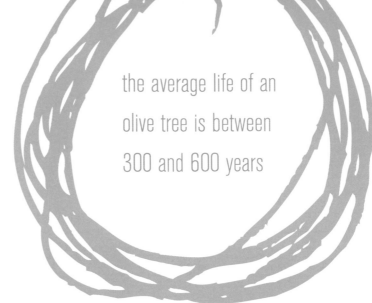

the average life of an
olive tree is between
300 and 600 years

1 jar or tin of 'turning' or black olives

1 jar or tin of green olives

200 g marinated white anchovies,
rinsed and drained

75 g caperberries in wine vinegar,
drained

1 tablespoon pink peppercorns

4 tablespoons olive oil

2 tablespoons sherry vinegar

1 tablespoon lemon juice

flat leaf parsley, to garnish

Drain the olives from the brine and place them in a bowl with the anchovies, caperberries and pink peppercorns.

Mix together the olive oil, sherry vinegar and lemon juice. Pour over the olives, tossing gently to mix. Leave to marinate for 20–30 minutes. Alternatively, cover and refrigerate for up to 3 days.

Serve at room temperature, garnished with flat leaf parsley.

Serves 4

olives with anchovies, caperberries and pink peppercorns

1 jar or tin of green olives

1 jar or tin of black olives

12 mild piquante peppers in brine

200 g crumbly white cheese, cut into cubes

150 g char-grilled artichokes in olive oil, drained and halved

6 basil leaves, plus extra to garnish

1 lemon

pinch of caster sugar

freshly ground black pepper

Drain the olives from the brine and place them in a bowl.

Drain the piquante peppers, then stuff each one with a cube of cheese. Add these to the olives with the artichokes. Tear in the basil leaves.

Take 3 tablespoons of the olive oil from the jar of artichokes and add 1 teaspoon of lemon zest (use a zester, if you have one – otherwise grate it finely). Squeeze the juice from the lemon and mix it into the olive oil with the pinch of sugar and a little freshly ground black pepper. Add to the olives and peppers, tossing gently to mix. Leave to marinate for 20–30 minutes.

Crumble any remaining cheese over the top and serve, garnished with extra basil leaves.

Serves 4

olives with artichokes and cheese-stuffed piquante peppers

1 jar or tin of black olives

2 tablespoons rice wine vinegar

1 tablespoon lime juice

3 tablespoons toasted sesame oil

1 teaspoon wasabi paste

20 g thinly sliced sushi ginger

**100 g smoked salmon,
sliced into strips**

**lime wedges and fresh dill,
to garnish**

Drain the black olives and place them in a bowl.

Mix together the rice wine vinegar, lime juice, toasted sesame oil and wasabi paste. Add this mixture to the olives with the sushi ginger and smoked salmon. Leave to marinate for 20–30 minutes. Alternatively, cover and refrigerate for up to 24 hours.

Serve at room temperature, garnished with lime wedges and dill sprigs.

Serves 4

wasabi and ginger olives with smoked salmon

warm lemon-thyme dressed olives

1 jar or tin of green olives

1 jar or tin of black olives

4 tablespoons olive oil

1 large garlic clove, thinly sliced

finely grated zest and juice of 1 lemon

1 teaspoon wholegrain mustard

freshly ground black pepper

3–4 sprigs fresh lemon thyme

slices of ciabatta bread, to serve

Serves 4

Drain the green and black olives from the brine and place them in a bowl.

Heat the olive oil in a small saucepan and add the garlic, frying it gently over a medium heat until light golden brown. Remove from the heat and add the lemon zest, lemon juice and wholegrain mustard. Season with a little black pepper.

Pour over the olives and toss together. Strip the leaves from the sprigs of lemon thyme and sprinkle them over the olives. Serve while warm, with lightly toasted ciabatta bread.

almond-stuffed olives with celery, fennel and rosemary

20 pitted queen olives in brine, drained

20 blanched almonds

4 tablespoons olive oil

2 celery sticks, thinly sliced

1 teaspoon fennel seeds

2 tablespoons orange juice

1 teaspoon roughly chopped fresh rosemary

Serves 4

Stuff each olive with a blanched almond and place them in a bowl.

Heat the olive oil and gently fry the celery and fennel seeds for about 2 minutes. Remove from the heat and add the orange juice.

Pour over the olives and toss together. Serve while warm, sprinkled with the rosemary.

250 g pitted black olives in brine, drained

6 anchovy fillets in olive oil, drained

1 garlic clove, crushed

4 tablespoons capers in brine, drained

small handful of flat leaf parsley, roughly chopped

3 tablespoons extra virgin olive oil

finely grated zest and juice of 1 lemon

Put the olives, anchovies, garlic, capers, parsley and olive oil into a blender or food processor and blend until smooth (though if you prefer a rough-textured tapenade, blend for less time).

Tip the tapenade into a bowl and add the lemon zest and lemon juice according to taste.

Serve as a dip or spread, served with crusty bread, crackers or vegetable crudités, or use to include in recipes. Keep in a jar in the refrigerator for up to 2 weeks.

Serves 4 black olive and anchovy tapenade

200 g pimiento-stuffed green olives in brine, drained

150 g sun-dried tomatoes in olive oil, drained

2 tablespoons capers in brine, drained

handful of basil leaves

3 tablespoons olive oil

freshly ground black pepper

Put the olives, tomatoes, capers, basil and olive oil into a blender or food processor and blend until smooth (though if you prefer a rough-textured tapenade, blend for less time).

Tip the tapenade into a bowl and season with freshly ground black pepper. Spoon into small pots and refrigerate for up to 1 week. Serve at room temperature for the best flavour.

Serves 4 green olive and tomato tapenade

150 g pitted black olives in brine, drained

150 g roasted red peppers in brine, drained

1 teaspoon finely chopped fresh red chilli

2 tablespoons extra virgin olive oil

freshly ground black pepper

savoury crackers, to serve

thin strips of roasted red pepper, snipped

fresh chives and black olives, to garnish

Put the black olives into a blender or food processor.

Make sure that the red peppers are thoroughly drained, patting them dry with kitchen paper. Chop them roughly and add to the blender or food processor with the chilli and olive oil. Blend until smooth.

Season with a little freshly ground black pepper. Spread on to crackers and serve, garnished with strips of roasted red pepper, snipped fresh chives and black olives. Alternatively, serve as a dip with warm pitta bread.

Serves 4

chilli, black olive and red pepper spread

200 g pitted black olives in brine, drained

1 garlic clove, crushed

small handful of fresh parsley

100 g whole hazelnuts

3 tablespoons olive oil

100 g Manchego cheese, finely grated

freshly ground black pepper

Put the olives, garlic and parsley into a blender or food processor.

Toast the whole hazelnuts in a dry frying pan for 2–3 minutes, then tip them into the blender or food processor and add the olive oil. Blend until smooth (though if you prefer a rough-textured tapenade, blend for less time).

Tip the mixture into a bowl and stir in the finely grated Manchego cheese. Season with freshly ground black pepper and serve with vegetable crudités, warm pitta bread or crusty fresh bread, or use to make bruschetta.

Serves 4

black olive, manchego and hazelnut tapenade

black olive, manchego and hazelnut bruschetta

Preheat the oven to 200°C/fan oven 180°C/Gas Mark 6.
Slice crusty fresh bread (a baton works well) into even pieces and spread them with the black olive, Manchego and hazelnut tapenade. Place on a baking sheet and top each one with sliced baby plum or cherry tomatoes and some finely chopped red onion. Drizzle with a little olive oil and bake for 8–10 minutes.
Serve, garnished with flat leaf parsley or basil leaves.

150 g pitted green olives in olive oil or brine, drained

150 g pitted black olives in olive oil or brine, drained

1 tablespoon lemongrass paste

1 tablespoon finely grated fresh root ginger

1 garlic clove, crushed

2 teaspoons finely chopped fresh red chilli

small handful of fresh coriander

2 tablespoons chilli-infused or extra virgin olive oil

freshly ground black pepper

chicory leaves (red and green, if available), or celery sticks, to serve

olives have been around for thousands of years and appeared in one of the earliest cookbooks ever discovered: the 2000-year-old text by a Roman named Apicius

Put the olives, lemongrass paste, ginger, garlic, chilli and coriander into a blender or food processor. Add the olive oil and blend until smooth (though if you prefer a rough-textured tapenade, blend for less time).

Spoon the tapenade into a bowl and season with a little black pepper, if needed. Serve with chicory leaves or celery sticks.

Serves 4

lemongrass, ginger and chilli tapenade

200 g pitted green olives in brine, drained

50 g pine nuts

2 tablespoons capers in brine, drained

handful of flat leaf parsley, roughly chopped

finely grated zest and juice of 1 small lemon

2 tablespoons olive oil

freshly ground black pepper

Put the olives into a blender or food processor.

Lightly toast the pine nuts in a dry frying pan until light golden brown. Tip them into the blender or food processor with the capers, parsley, lemon zest, lemon juice and olive oil. Blend until smooth (though if you prefer a rough-textured tapenade, blend for less time), then season to taste with freshly ground black pepper.

Use as a dip or spread, or try using the tapenade in this easy fish dish.

Serves 4

lemon, green olive, pine nut and parsley tapenade

roasted fish with lemon, green olive, pine nut and parsley tapenade

Preheat the oven to 190°C/fan oven 170°C/Gas Mark 5.
Arrange 4 x 150 g fillets of haddock, cod loin or salmon in a roasting dish and spread 1–2 tablespoons of the lemon, green olive, pine nut and parsley tapenade on top of each one. Place a small bunch of cherry tomatoes on-the-vine on top of each fish fillet, then roast for 18–20 minutes.
Serve, garnished with parsley and lemon wedges.

2 large yellow peppers, halved and deseeded

200 g pitted green olives in brine, drained

1 tablespoon olive oil

2 teaspoons anchovy paste

50 g low fat soft cheese with garlic and herbs

freshly ground black pepper

vegetable crudités, to serve

Preheat the grill. Arrange the peppers, skin sides up, on the grill rack. Grill them until the skin is blackened and charred, then leave in a warm place for 20 minutes for the skins to loosen. Do this by closing the grill compartment, so that they cool in the steamy atmosphere, or put them into a large food bag, sealing it closed.

Peel the grilled peppers, then put them into a blender or food processor with the olives, olive oil, anchovy paste and soft cheese. Season with black pepper and blend until smooth (though if you prefer a rougher texture, blend for less time).

Spoon the dip into a bowl and serve with fresh vegetable crudités.

Serves 4

green olive and grilled yellow pepper dip

olive trees are ready to harvest from the age of three but attain their highest yields from the eighth year onwards

4 soft flour tortillas

2 tablespoons olive oil

200 g pitted green olives in brine, drained

2 ripe avocados, halved, pitted and peeled

1 tomato, skinned, deseeded and chopped

2 teaspoons finely chopped green chilli

2 tablespoons chopped fresh coriander

salt and freshly ground black pepper

juice of ½ lime

lime wedges and coriander sprigs, to garnish

Preheat the oven to 200°C/fan oven 180°C/Gas Mark 6.

Brush each tortilla with a little olive oil, then cut each one into 8 wedges, using a pair of scissors. Arrange them on two baking sheets. Bake for 10–12 minutes, until crisp and light golden brown.

Meanwhile, use some kitchen paper to pat the olives dry, then chop them finely.

Mash the avocados with a fork, then add the olives, tomato, chilli and coriander. Season with a little salt, pepper and lime juice.

Spoon the guacamole into a serving bowl and garnish with lime wedges and coriander sprigs. Serve with the tortilla wedges.

Serves 4

green olive and coriander guacamole

PARMESAN CURLS

150 g Parmesan cheese, finely grated

TAPENADE

150 g pitted black olives in brine, drained

150 g roasted peppers in olive oil, drained

2 teaspoons finely chopped fresh green chilli

100 g blanched almonds

small handful of fresh parsley

freshly ground black pepper

Preheat a hot grill. Place heaped tablespoons of the Parmesan cheese, spaced apart, on to a baking sheet. Flatten them down slightly. Grill for 1–2 minutes, until melted and beginning to brown. Remove from the baking sheet with a palette knife while still warm and place on a rolling pin, so that they cool in slight curls. Repeat until all the cheese is used up.

For the tapenade, put the olives, roasted peppers, chilli, almonds and parsley into a blender or food processor. Add 2 tablespoons of oil from the jar of peppers and blend until smooth. Tip into a bowl and season with black pepper. Serve with the Parmesan curls.

Serves 4

parmesan curls with olive and almond tapenade

200 g pitted black olives in brine, drained

150 g sun-blush or sun-dried tomatoes in olive oil, drained

1 garlic clove, crushed

generous pinch of dried red chilli flakes

handful of basil leaves

freshly ground black pepper

Put the olives, tomatoes, garlic, chilli flakes and basil into a blender or food processor. Add 2 tablespoons of the oil from the jar of tomatoes and blend until smooth (though if you prefer a rough-textured tapenade, blend for less time).

Serve with crackers or crudités, or use some to make these tasty cheese whirls.

Serves 4

red-hot tapenade

red-hot tapenade manchego whirls

Makes 16 Preheat the oven to 220°C/fan oven 200°C/Gas Mark 7. Unroll a thawed 320 g frozen puff pastry sheet and spread 4 tablespoons of the red-hot tapenade over the surface. Sprinkle with 100 g finely grated Manchego cheese and roll up from the short end. Cut into 16 slices and lay them flat on a greased baking sheet. Bake for approximately 15 minutes until golden brown.
Serve while warm, garnished with fresh basil leaves.

TAPENADE

250 g pitted black olives in brine, drained

1 garlic clove, crushed

3 tablespoons capers in brine, drained

2 tablespoons olive oil

1 teaspoon finely chopped fresh red chilli

SALSA

3 tomatoes, finely chopped

¼ cucumber, finely chopped

½ small red onion, finely chopped

2 tablespoons chopped fresh coriander

salt

GUACAMOLE

2 ripe avocados, halved, pitted and peeled

1 tomato, skinned, deseeded and chopped

freshly ground black pepper

squeeze of lime juice

tortilla chips, to serve

when the tradition of tapas was born, the first and simplest type was a slice of bread with olives

Make the tapenade by putting the olives, garlic, capers, olive oil and chilli into a blender or food processor. Blend until smooth.

Make the salsa by mixing together the tomatoes, cucumber, red onion and chopped fresh coriander. Season with a little salt.

Make the guacamole by mashing the avocados, then mix in the tomato. Season with freshly ground black pepper and a squeeze of lime juice.

Layer the mixtures in a glass jar or attractive serving dishes, salsa first, then guacamole and finally tapenade. Serve with tortilla chips.

Serves 4

tapenade, guacamole and salsa three-layer dip

1 small red onion, finely chopped

2 tablespoons red or white wine vinegar

pinch of sugar

150 g pitted green olives in olive oil or brine, drained

150 g pitted black olives in olive oil or brine, drained

410 g can cannellini beans, rinsed and drained

160 g can tuna fish in oil or water, drained and mashed with a fork

1 tablespoon chopped fresh parsley

salt and freshly ground black pepper

parsley sprigs, to garnish

Melba toast and extra black and green olives, to serve

Put the red onion into a bowl with the vinegar and sugar and set aside to marinate for at least 10 minutes.

Meanwhile, put half the green olives and half the black olives into a blender or food processor with the cannellini beans and blend until smooth. Tip into a bowl. Chop the remaining olives roughly, then add these to the blended mixture with the mashed tuna, chopped parsley and most of the drained onion.

Season with a little salt and freshly ground black pepper. Transfer to a serving bowl and sprinkle with the reserved red onion. Garnish with parsley and serve with Melba toast.

Serves 4   olive and tuna pâté

2 tablespoons olive oil

1 small aubergine, finely chopped

4 spring onions, finely chopped

150 g mushrooms, finely chopped

150 g pitted green olives in olive oil or brine, drained

150 g pitted black olives in olive oil or brine, drained

1 tablespoon chopped fresh oregano or parsley

salt and freshly ground black pepper

savoury crackers or crusty bread, to serve

piquillo peppers or roasted red peppers in brine, drained, to garnish

green and black olives, to garnish

Heat the olive oil in a large non-stick frying pan and add the aubergine, spring onions and mushrooms. Fry gently over a low heat until very soft (about 10–15 minutes), adding a splash of water if needed. Cool.

Put the aubergine mixture into a blender or food processor with the olives and oregano or parsley. Blend until smooth (though if you prefer a rough-textured tapenade, blend for less time). Season to taste.

Spread the tapenade on to savoury crackers or crusty bread. Serve, garnished with strips of piquillo peppers or roasted red peppers and extra olives.

Serves 4

olive, mushroom and aubergine tapenade

200 g pitted black olives in brine or olive oil, drained

220 g jar whole piquillo peppers, drained

2 tablespoons capers in brine, drained

handful of basil leaves, plus extra, to garnish

3 tablespoons olive oil

12 thin slices crusty bread, toasted

150 g goat's cheese, sliced

olive oil, for drizzling

freshly ground black pepper

Put the olives and piquillo peppers into a blender or food processor with the capers, basil leaves and olive oil and blend until smooth (though if you prefer a rough-textured tapenade, blend for less time).

Tip the tapenade into a bowl and season with freshly ground black pepper.

Preheat the oven to 190°C/fan oven 170°C/Gas Mark 5.

Spread some of the tapenade on to the slices of crusty bread and arrange them on a baking sheet. Put a piece of goat's cheese on top, drizzle with a little olive oil and season with black pepper. Bake for 10-12 minutes.

Serve, garnished with fresh basil leaves.

Serves 4

black olive tapenade and goat's cheese croustades

200 g pitted green olives in brine, drained

1 large carrot, finely grated

100 g houmous

1 teaspoon black onion seeds (optional)

1 teaspoon sesame seeds

1 tablespoon extra virgin olive oil

4 white pittas

20 g butter, melted

sea salt, for sprinkling

2 sprigs fresh rosemary

Put the olives into a blender or food processor with the grated carrot and houmous. Blend until smooth. Tip the mixture into a serving bowl.

Toast the black onion seeds (if using) and sesame seeds in a dry frying pan for 1–2 minutes, until fragrant. Stir most of these through the olive mixture. Drizzle the olive oil on top and sprinkle with the reserved onion seeds and sesame seeds.

Preheat the grill. Place the pittas on the grill rack and brush them with the melted butter. Sprinkle a little sea salt on top, and snip the fresh rosemary sprigs over them. Warm under the grill for about 1 minute.

Serve with the houmous.

Serves 4

green olive and carrot houmous with rosemary and sea salt pitta

the olive branch has for thousands of years been used as a symbol of peace and goodwill

2 large carrots, grated

1 small onion, finely chopped

1 garlic clove, crushed

100 g dried red lentils

450 ml vegetable stock

100 g pitted green olives in olive oil or brine, drained

1 teaspoon ground cumin

1 teaspoon ground coriander

pinch of dried chilli flakes

freshly ground black pepper

20 g butter

4 mini naan breads

1 teaspoon whole cumin seeds

Put the carrots, onion, garlic and red lentils into a saucepan with the vegetable stock. Bring to the boil, then reduce the heat and simmer, partially covered, for about 40 minutes, until the lentils are tender and the liquid has almost evaporated. Drain thoroughly and set aside to cool in a colander or large sieve.

Put the olives into a blender or food processor with the lentil mixture. Add the ground cumin, coriander and dried chilli flakes and blend until smooth. Season with a little black pepper, then spoon the mixture into a serving bowl.

Preheat the grill. Spread the butter over the naan breads and sprinkle the cumin seeds over the top. Grill for 1–2 minutes until lightly toasted.

Serve with the dhal.

Serves 4

indian-spiced olive and lentil dhal

pepper-stuffed olives in parmesan panko breadcrumbs

24 pitted queen olives

1 roasted red pepper in brine, drained and sliced into thin strips

50 g plain flour

2 eggs, beaten

75 g Japanese panko breadcrumbs

50 g finely grated Parmesan cheese

sunflower oil, for shallow frying

freshly ground black pepper

Serves 4

Drain the queen olives from the brine and stuff each one with a strip of red pepper.

Put the flour into a small bowl and the eggs into a second bowl. Tip the breadcrumbs and Parmesan cheese into a third bowl, mixing them together well. Roll the olives in the flour, then dip them in the beaten egg and coat in the breadcrumb mixture.

Heat the sunflower oil in a small frying pan and shallow fry the olives, in batches, until golden and crispy. Drain on kitchen paper, and serve while hot.

olive nibbles

200 g black olives in olive oil or brine, drained

12 baby plum tomatoes, halved

½ cucumber, cut into chunks

200 g crumbly white cheese, cut into chunks

1 teaspoon finely grated lemon zest

juice of 1 lemon

2 tablespoons chopped fresh mint

4 tablespoons extra virgin olive oil

pinch of sugar

salt and freshly ground black pepper

Serves 4

Put the olives into a serving bowl and add the plum tomatoes, cucumber and cheese.

For the dressing, whisk together the lemon zest, lemon juice, mint and olive oil with a pinch of sugar, salt and freshly ground black pepper. Drizzle over the olive mixture, then serve.

olive trees can live for
more than 1500 years
and grow to a maximum
of 50 feet tall

2 large sweet potatoes, scrubbed
and cut into chunks

2 tablespoons olive oil

150 g pitted green olives in olive oil,
drained

150 g pitted 'turning' or black olives
in olive oil, drained

1 teaspoon whole cumin seeds

¼ teaspoon dried chilli flakes

2 tablespoons lemon juice

Preheat the oven to 200°C/fan oven 180°C/Gas Mark 6.

Put the sweet potato chunks into a roasting tin and add the olive oil, tossing to coat. Roast for about 25 minutes, turning once, until tender.

Meanwhile, warm the olives in a saucepan with 2 tablespoons of oil from the jar. Add the cumin seeds and dried chilli flakes. Heat for 1–2 minutes, then add the lemon juice and set aside to cool.

Mix the sweet potato and olives together, then serve.

Serves 4

mixed cumin and chilli-spiced olives with roasted sweet potato

1 jar or tin of green olives

1 jar or tin of black olives

**1 large ripe mango, pitted, peeled
and cut into chunks**

**½ small melon, deseeded and cut
into small chunks**

Drain the olives from the brine and place them in a bowl.

50 g prepared pomegranate

Mix together the mango, melon and pomegranate with the lime or lemon juice.

2 tablespoons lime or lemon juice

Add the fruit to the olives and mix together gently.

mint leaves, to garnish

Serve, garnished with fresh mint leaves.

Serves 4   olives with mango, melon and
pomegranate

24 black olives in brine or olive oil

12 cherry tomatoes, quartered

6 baby sweet peppers (red, yellow and orange), halved and deseeded

2 sprigs fresh rosemary

2–3 tablespoons olive oil

freshly ground black pepper

Preheat the oven to 190°C/fan oven 170°C/Gas Mark 5.

Drain the olives and slice them thinly. Mix them with the cherry tomatoes.

Arrange the peppers, cut sides up, in a roasting tin. Sprinkle with a little olive oil and roast for 10 minutes.

Spoon the tomatoes and olives into the peppers. Strip the leaves from the rosemary sprigs and sprinkle them over the top. Season with black pepper and roast for 5–10 more minutes. Cool for a few minutes, then serve.

Serves 4

150 g thick, creamy natural yogurt

¼ cucumber, finely chopped

2 tablespoons chopped fresh mint

2 large skinless, boneless chicken
breasts, each cut into 8 pieces

2 tablespoons plain flour

1 egg

100 g dried breadcrumbs

1 teaspoon smoked paprika

olive oil, for shallow frying

150 g green olives in olive oil, drained

150 g black olives in olive oil, drained

salt and freshly ground black pepper

Mix together the yogurt, cucumber and mint and set to one side.

Roll the pieces of chicken in the plain flour, seasoning them with a little salt and pepper.

Beat the egg in a shallow bowl with 1 tablespoon of cold water. Put the breadcrumbs on to a plate and mix in the smoked paprika. Dip the chicken pieces into the egg, then coat them in breadcrumbs.

Heat the olive oil in a non-stick frying pan and gently shallow fry the chicken for 8–10 minutes until golden brown and cooked through. Drain on kitchen paper, then mix with the olives. Spoon into a dish and serve, accompanied by the mint and cucumber dip.

Serves 4   smoked chicken paprika and olives

olives are renowned for
their nutritional properties,
and the olive stone can
be used as an exfoliator

1 stalk lemongrass, finely sliced

2 teaspoons freshly grated root ginger

1 small red chilli, deseeded and thinly sliced

1 kaffir lime leaf

300 ml vegetable stock

450 g mussels, scrubbed

200 g squid rings

150 g pitted green olives in olive oil or brine, drained

150 g pitted 'turning' or black olives in olive oil or brine, drained

chopped fresh coriander, to garnish

Put the lemongrass, ginger, chilli, lime leaf and stock into a large saucepan. Cover and simmer for 5 minutes.

Add the mussels (discarding any that do not close when tapped) and squid to the saucepan. Cover and cook for 3–4 minutes, until the mussels open. (Discard any that do not open.)

Remove from the heat, add the olives, then spoon into serving dishes. Serve, garnished with chopped fresh coriander.

Serves 4 fragrant thai seafood with black and green olives

olive and ricotta filo pastry twists

12 pitted queen olives in brine or
olive oil, drained

50 g ricotta or cream cheese

3 sheets filo pastry, thawed if frozen

50 g butter, melted

freshly ground black pepper

sweet chilli dipping sauce, to serve

Serves 4

Preheat the oven to 200°C/fan oven 180°C/Gas Mark 6. Lightly grease a baking sheet.

Stuff each olive with the ricotta or cream cheese.

Unroll the sheets of filo pastry and brush each one lightly with melted butter, placing them on top of each other. Cut into 12 squares.

Place an olive on top of each square and season with a little black pepper. Gather the pastry around each olive into a twist, then place on the prepared baking sheet and brush with any remaining melted butter. Bake for 12–15 minutes, until light golden brown. Serve with sweet chilli dipping sauce.

olive-stuffed eggs paprika

4 large eggs

12 pimiento-stuffed green olives in
brine, drained

75 g cream cheese with garlic
and herbs

smoked paprika,
for sprinkling

fresh parsley sprigs, to garnish

Serves 4

Boil the eggs in simmering water for 12 minutes. Plunge them into cold water and let them cool.

Reserve 4 olives for garnish, then finely chop the rest. Mix these with the cream cheese.

Shell the eggs, then slice them in half and carefully remove the yolks. Add the yolks to the cream cheese mixture and mash them in with a fork. Pile this mixture back into the empty egg whites.

Sprinkle the eggs with smoked paprika and serve, garnished with the reserved olives, cut in half, and fresh parsley sprigs.

12 black olives in olive oil or brine, drained and halved

50 g Serrano ham, thinly sliced

2 tablespoons lemon-infused or basil-infused olive oil

4 baby avocados, halved, peeled and pitted

few drops of balsamic vinegar

freshly ground black pepper

basil leaves, to garnish

Mix together the black olives, Serrano ham and lemon or basil-infused olive oil.

Arrange the avocado halves on a serving platter and spoon the olive mixture into them. Season with a little freshly ground black pepper.

Serve, sprinkled with a few drops of balsamic vinegar and garnished with fresh basil leaves.

Serves 4

baby avocados stuffed with serrano ham and black olives

250 g lean minced lamb

2 tablespoons finely chopped red onion

1 teaspoon ground cumin

1 teaspoon ground coriander

1 medium carrot, grated

1 tablespoon chopped fresh mint

salt and freshly ground black pepper

2 tablespoons olive oil

3 tablespoons sweet chilli sauce

1 jar or tin of green olives, drained

mint leaves, to garnish

Put the lamb, red onion, ground cumin and ground coriander into a mixing bowl with the grated carrot and mint. Season with salt and pepper and mix together thoroughly. Form into about 30 small meatballs – it helps if you have wet hands for this.

Heat the olive oil in a non-stick frying pan and gently fry the meatballs for 12–15 minutes, turning occasionally – though do this gently to avoid breaking them up.

Drain the meatballs on kitchen paper, then put them in a serving bowl and spoon the chilli sauce on top. Place the olives among the meatballs and serve at once, garnished with fresh mint leaves.

Serves 4

green olives with chilli lamb meatballs

36 pimiento-stuffed green olives

24 cooked, peeled, tail-on
tiger prawns

24 baby plum tomatoes

2 teaspoons fresh lemon
thyme leaves

Thread three olives, two prawns and two tomatoes alternately on to 12 skewers or wooden sticks.

2 tablespoons lemon juice

4 tablespoons olive oil

Mix together the thyme leaves, lemon juice, olive oil and mustard. Drizzle over the skewers.

1 teaspoon mild mustard

freshly ground black pepper

Serve at once, sprinkled with a little black pepper.

Serves 4

tiger prawns skewered with olives and tomatoes

Drain the olives from the brine and place them in a bowl.

Heat a non-stick frying pan and add the slices of chorizo. Cook over a medium-high heat for 3–4 minutes, until the fat begins to run.

Meanwhile, use a melon baller to remove the flesh from the melon, and add to the olives with the Manchego cheese. (Alternatively, you could just cut the melon into chunks.)

Remove the chorizo from the heat and tip on to the olive mixture. Serve at once, garnished with fresh basil leaves.

1 jar or tin of queen olives

150 g chorizo sausage, sliced

½ orange-fleshed cantaloupe melon

150 g Manchego cheese, cut into chunks

basil leaves, to garnish

Serves 4

green olives with manchego, chorizo and melon

the Phoenicians brought the olive tree to Spain, but it was under the Romans that olives were first cultivated on a grand scale

150 g pitted green olives in brine, drained

150 g pitted black olives in brine, drained

3 tablespoons lemon-infused or extra virgin olive oil

finely grated zest and juice of 1 orange

350 g bulgur wheat

600 ml hot vegetable stock

½ cucumber, finely chopped

6 spring onions, finely chopped

3 tomatoes, deseeded and finely chopped

2 tablespoons chopped fresh parsley

2 tablespoons chopped fresh mint

salt and freshly ground black pepper

Chop the olives roughly and tip them into a serving bowl. Add the olive oil, orange zest and orange juice and stir to mix.

Put the bulgur wheat into a saucepan and add the hot stock. Simmer for 5–6 minutes until swollen and tender. Drain and cool for 15–20 minutes.

Tip the bulgur wheat into the olive mixture and add the cucumber, spring onions, tomatoes, parsley and mint.

Season and serve while barely warm, or cool completely and serve as a side salad or as part of a packed lunch or picnic.

Serves 4   olive tabbouleh

serrano-wrapped scallops with piquillo peppers and olives

12 oregano or basil leaves

12 scallops

6 slices Serrano ham, cut in half

1 tablespoon olive oil

3 tablespoons full-bodied sherry

pinch of vegetable or chicken stock powder

200 g black olives in olive oil or brine, drained

100 g piquillo peppers in olive oil or brine, drained

oregano or basil leaves, to garnish

Serves 4

Place an oregano leaf or basil leaf on top of each scallop and wrap half a slice of Serrano ham around each one.

Heat the olive oil in a frying pan and add the Serrano ham-wrapped scallops, cooking them for about 2 minutes before turning them over to cook the other side.

Add the sherry, 2 tablespoons of water and the pinch of stock powder. Simmer for 2–3 minutes to reduce the liquid a little.

Add the black olives and piquillo peppers to the scallops, then spoon into a serving dish and serve while warm, garnished with oregano or basil leaves.

black olives with watermelon, pistachios and halloumi

1 jar or tin of black olives

1 wedge of watermelon, peeled and cut into chunks

80 g shelled pistachio nuts

200 g halloumi cheese, sliced

3 tablespoons lemon-infused olive oil

Serves 4

Drain the olives from the brine and place them in a bowl. Add the chunks of watermelon and mix together gently.

Heat a non-stick frying pan and toast the pistachio nuts for 2–3 minutes to bring out their flavour. Tip them out of the pan and wipe it clean with kitchen paper. Next, add the slices of halloumi cheese to the frying pan and cook them, without adding any oil, until lightly browned, turning them over to cook the other side. Transfer to sheets of kitchen paper to cool for a few moments.

Break up the halloumi cheese into chunks and scatter them over the olives and watermelon. Serve, drizzled with the lemon-infused olive oil.

recipe index